Copyright © 2020 Chris Gibbs

First Edition

ISBN 978-1-9996363-4-0

Published by Inner Version Ltd
www.innerversion.com

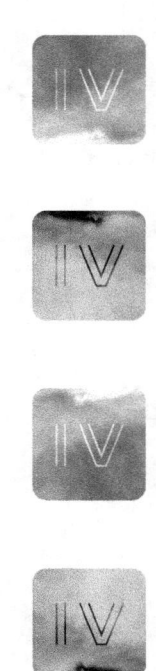

LXXX — MOUNTAIN RISING

I. Guiding stones
    Positioned in a distant time
Are hidden from afar.

II. The base of the mountain
    Presents a vista as inspiring
        As the summit.

LXXXI — THRESHOLD ELEVATION

I. Creative sparks
    Accumulate at the gate
    To amplify their full potential.

II. Individuality expresses
    Judgement in the deepest clarity
    From the art absorbed entirely.

LXXXII — DIFFERENCE INTERPLAYED

I. Material that exists
    Makes a difference;
Material that makes a difference
    Exists.

II. Light requires dark
    For definition;
Dark requires light
    For illumination.

III. The unfolding of the universe
    Exposes difference;
The interplay of difference
    Discovers unity.

LXXXIII — OPPOSITE CONTAINMENT

I. The empty vessel
    Cradles the fullness of space.

II. The sealed chamber
    Conveys the opening of time.

III. The barren desert
    Bears the winds of transformation.

IV. The forest clearing
    Holds the opportunity for life.

LXXXIV — GREATNESS UNEXPRESSED

I.   Connection to the ancient
        Rediscovers smallness of living;
        Simplicity endures.

II.   Behind the falls
        And rises of the eons,
        Persists the great unchanged.

LXXXV – IMPULSIVE WIDENESS

I. Patience wells from patience,
   Divides the ancient chasm.

II. Humbleness submits to humbleness,
    Grows the light embracing.

LXXXVI — CONTINUOUS SOUL

I. The dormant soul
    Stirs and wakes
        In the middle of the all.

II. The life awakened
    Senses the continuous
        Projections of the self.

LXXXVII — TIME INHERITANCE

I. Running through the generations,
    Surface time
        Flows by.

II. Ancient movement
    Is revealed, the inner
        Child awakens.

LXXXVIII — UPLIFTING SELECTION

I. Uplifting intention
Draws in the magical,
    Steers around the mechanical.

II. Experience selection
    Feels the pulses coursing
        Through the universe,
    Captures the sparks intended.

LXXXIX — SEAMLESS WONDER

I. The understated thought of old
 Transforms with seamless lift
  Into excitement of the new.

II. The act of genuine kindness
 Returns without awaited answer
  To elation of the start.

XC — UNLIFTED ELEGANCE

I. The magic transforms
    Upon lifting the veil.

II. The mystery falls
    Upon the effortless silence.

XCI — IDEAL COMPARISON

I. The cycle of perpetual shift
 Between attachment and detachment
  Heals the common view,
  Restores the vibrant ideal.

II. The absence of a standard baseline
  Yields the full creative power.

XCII — ENTIRE APPROVAL

I. Deviation from internal harmony
    Appreciates the inward path.

II. Acceptance of unrealised awakening
    Initiates the brighter culture.

XCIII — TRANSLUCENT ADORATION

I.   The collected light of a thousand
            Suns — fascinates the special
            Wavelengths of inner being.

II.   The passionate display of deep
            Internal colour — shines a lantern
            Guiding to the universal source.

XCIV — INVITED OPENING

I. The open window
      To the farthest reaches of the soul
  Illuminates the darkest parts,
      Kindles the warmth internal.

II. The gentle invitation
      To the corner of the world
  Shines through the bustling crowds,
      Beckons to the eyes receptive.

XCV — IDEAL CHANNEL

I. The deep unbounded stream
    Flows with light and dark,
    Whirls with relevance and irrelevance
According to desire.

II. Meditation gently focused
On the neutral point
    Improves ability to discern,
    Prolongs the open channel.

XCVI — SURFACING CREATION

I.   Approaching sense of depth
        Arises out of stillness.

II.   The hazy outline
        Shapes the deep conception
        In retreat from the surface.

III.   The beckoning ideas
        Respond from the depths
        As echoes in time profound.

XCVII — INNER REASSURANCE

I. The deeper calling
    For the task inventive
        Can be trusted.

II. The positive intent
    Rewards in ways mysterious
        To the external.

XCVIII — SUBJECTIVE DEPTH

I.   In the shallow waters
        Of rational thought,
        Objectivity gives way
            To the search beneath the sand.

II.   Bubbles rising
        From the murky depths relinquish
        Rationality on their unique
            Ascent to the surface.

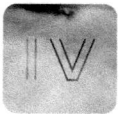

XCIX — PERSONAL RESONANCE

I. The unique accretion
   Of references to the eternal
       Chimes with inner wonder.

II. The art revisited
    Reveals the deeper resonance.

C — INDIVIDUAL PALETTE

I.   Every personal preference
        Of colour, shape or form
       Reaches from a place
           Beyond comprehension.

II.   Creation arising
        From the limited palette
        Breaks through the limiting sphere
           Of choice indefinite.

CI — IMPERFECT DISRUPTION

I. The obstacle placed in the path —
    Frustration transforms creatively
        Into gratitude.

II. The injection of randomness —
    Illuminates the avenues
        In the search for resonance.

CII — RESTARTING POINT

I. Highlights of the art
    Owe full dependence
    On events precise;
Regret subsides.

II. Every chosen point
    Of opportunity to ascend
    Becomes the new foundation;
        Enjoyment rises.

CIII — STRENGTH ASCENDING

I. The myriad throws of darkness
   Brightly tempt from behind the shadows.

II. The narrow shaft of light
    Submits darkly the path of ascension.

CIV — MOUNTAIN MEDITATION

I. Awareness during the ascent
    To peak experience increases
    Freedom, clarity amplifies
        At the summit.

II. Meditation on the high
    Plateau postpones the subtle
        Shift to automatic staleness.

III. Yielding to the slow
        Descent of inactivity renews
    Ambition in the darkness
        For the mountain rise.

CV — IMPERFECT ASCENSION

I.   Expectation for the path
       Of perfect definition
       Increases fatigue,
Lowers vitality.

II.   Aspiration for the plane
       Of high sophistication
Removes indifference,
      Elevates existence.

CVI — RESPONSIBLE FLOW

I. Duty beckons,
   Purpose is gained.

II. Responsibility subsides,
    The world relaxes.

CVII — INDIVIDUAL INSPIRATION

I. The leader esteemed
    Conceives a path to serve
        As inspiration,
    Not to imitate precisely.

II. The follower inspired
    Equals the devotion and sincerity
    For individual life.

CVIII — DESTINY INTERNAL

I. Individual destiny
    Is to be discovered
        Beyond imagination,
    Not to be chosen.

II. The example and the revolutionary,
The martyr and the prophet —
    Dreams of becoming escape
        Into the ideals of the masses.

III. True desire
    Is in response
        To the calling
        From your inner version.

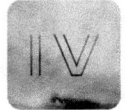

CIX — CLEAR AUTONOMY

I. Individuality requires
    Thoughtful discipline.

II. Clarity deserves
    Unbounded satisfaction.

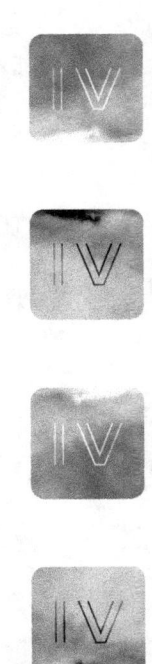

CX — INNER VISION

I. Panoramic vistas
    Revolve around the central point.

II. External projections
    Already exist within.

III. The life unique
    Expresses from reality internal.

CXI — RIGHTFUL CELEBRATION

I. Expression of creative freedom
    Steps into the limelight.

II. Desire for restrictive fame
    Dissolves beneath the shadows.

CXII – SHARED ACHIEVEMENT

I. Personal gain
    Withdraws from public view;
Shared achievement
    Celebrates the full dependence.

II. Contribution aims
    To be discovered
        In the distance.

CXIII — ALLEVIATING TIME

I. The clasp of time precision
    Sways and falls
        Into the haze descended.

II. The pause of ancient rhythm
    Arises from the mist
        As the lights of gentle freedom.

CXIV — NO EXPECTATION

I. Sensation of the stillness
    Blooms to full awareness;
    Memory suspends.

II. Decay in ancient structure
    Reveals the lack of expectation;
    Elation emerges.

CXV — ALMOST UNIVERSAL

I.   To dwell among the stars
        Is to find the stillness
          On the cusp of life's desire.

II.   To traverse the inner worlds
        Is to share the progress
          In the view of eyes awakened.

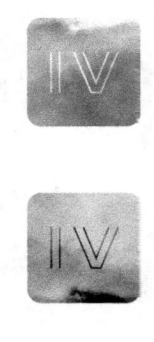

CXVI — NEVERENDING RESOLVE

I.   Each satisfying segment
        Of the neverending puzzle
        Contains the hidden fortune.

II.   The single piece
        Resolved in depths eternal
        Attracts the lifelong passion.

CXVII — THE CATALYST

I. Life is revitalised —
   Praising tales of wonder.

II. The flourishing unique
    Ignites the sparks untold.

III. The worldly interest
     Increases rate of joy.

IV. Excitement overflows,
    Thoughts are focused inward.

CXVIII — INWARD ELEVATION

I. The stream of outer prejudice
    Is strengthened in conformity
    By the common masses.

II. The path to inner wholeness
    Is raised above the tide
    By the individual.

CXIX — ETERNAL CONTACT

I. Ideas of value
    From the great eternal source
    Stream selectively in person.

II. Complacency accommodates
    To the shall-nots of the past;
The timeless view discovers
    Judgement of ideas in themselves.

III. The touch of the individual
    Renews the whole world.

LXXX —	MOUNTAIN RISING
LXXXI —	THRESHOLD ELEVATION
LXXXII —	DIFFERENCE INTERPLAYED
LXXXIII —	OPPOSITE CONTAINMENT
LXXXIV —	GREATNESS UNEXPRESSED
LXXXV —	IMPULSIVE WIDENESS
LXXXVI —	CONTINUOUS SOUL
LXXXVII —	TIME INHERITANCE
LXXXVIII —	UPLIFTING SELECTION
LXXXIX —	SEAMLESS WONDER
XC —	UNLIFTED ELEGANCE
XCI —	IDEAL COMPARISON
XCII —	ENTIRE APPROVAL
XCIII —	TRANSLUCENT ADORATION
XCIV —	INVITED OPENING
XCV —	IDEAL CHANNEL
XCVI —	SURFACING CREATION
XCVII —	INNER REASSURANCE
XCVIII —	SUBJECTIVE DEPTH
XCIX —	PERSONAL RESONANCE

C —	INDIVIDUAL PALETTE
CI —	IMPERFECT DISRUPTION
CII —	RESTARTING POINT
CIII —	STRENGTH ASCENDING
CIV —	MOUNTAIN MEDITATION
CV —	IMPERFECT ASCENSION
CVI —	RESPONSIBLE FLOW
CVII —	INDIVIDUAL INSPIRATION
CVIII —	DESTINY INTERNAL
CIX —	CLEAR AUTONOMY
CX —	INNER VISION
CXI —	RIGHTFUL CELEBRATION
CXII —	SHARED ACHIEVEMENT
CXIII —	ALLEVIATING TIME
CXIV —	NO EXPECTATION
CXV —	ALMOST UNIVERSAL
CXVI —	NEVERENDING RESOLVE
CXVII —	THE CATALYST
CXVIII —	INWARD ELEVATION
CXIX —	ETERNAL CONTACT

www.ingramcontent.com/pod-product-compliance
Lightning Source LLC
Chambersburg PA
CBHW071916070526
44583CB00016B/2020